Top Ten

TOP TEN
REASONS
AUTHORS
SHOULD
CREATE
AUDIOBOOKS
B Alan Bourgeois
AWARD-WINNING AUTHOR
AWARD-WINNING SPEAKER
AUTHOR ADVOCATE
THE AUTHOR'S
GUIDE TO
AUDIOBOOK
MASTERY

Top Ten Reasons Authors Should Create Audiobooks

ISBN: 979-8-8691-3805-7

Publisher: Bourgeois Media & Consulting (BourgeoisMedia.com)

BOURGEOIS
MEDIA & CONSULTING

Introduction

Embarking on the journey of transforming your masterpiece into an audiobook may initially feel like a daunting challenge for many authors. Moving from print versions to eBooks was a leap, and now venturing into the realm of audiobooks may seem like uncharted territory, challenging you to step out of your comfort zone. I've been there, just like many authors, hesitant to embrace this new medium. However, consider this guide your compass to navigate the world of audiobooks, understand their significance in publishing, and unlock a realm of increased income and exposure for your work. Think of it as an exciting expedition into unexplored horizons where listeners eagerly discover and relish your creations. This guide serves as a fundamental companion to unravel the essence and value of audiobooks. Recognizing the ever-evolving landscape of publishing over the past 50 years, we acknowledge the emergence of new opportunities like NFTs and evolving methods of sharing electronic files. While change is constant, this book aims to provide you, the author, with the confidence and ease to transition your book into the dynamic realm of audiobooks. Embrace this journey and let the excitement of reaching a broader audience through the magic of spoken words propel you forward!

Contents

1
Expanding Horizons

The Power of Audiobooks in Reaching Diverse Audiences

In the ever-evolving landscape of literature, authors are constantly exploring new avenues to connect with readers. One such avenue that has gained significant traction is the world of audiobooks. Beyond the traditional printed page, audiobooks offer a unique and compelling way to engage audiences, particularly those who prefer listening over reading. In this blog post, we'll delve into the concept of expanded audience reach through audiobooks, exploring the ways in which this medium broadens a book's accessibility and appeal.

Embracing Diversity in Audience Preferences

The beauty of audiobooks lies in their ability to cater to diverse audience preferences. While some readers relish the tangible feel of a book in their hands, others find solace in the immersive experience of listening to a narrated story. Audiobooks extend an olive branch to individuals with varying preferences, breaking down barriers and making literary content more inclusive.

Audiobooks and Accessibility

One of the most significant advantages of audiobooks is their contribution to accessibility. For individuals with visual impairments or learning disabilities, audiobooks provide an alternative means of consuming content. The narration brings stories to life, offering an auditory journey that transcends the limitations of traditional text.

Broadening Reach Beyond Reading

Audiobooks go beyond the confines of reading, allowing audiences to multitask while immersing themselves in a story. Commuting, exercising, or doing household chores—audiobooks accompany listeners in various facets of their lives. This versatility ensures that your book becomes a companion in situations where reading may not be practical.

Examples of Successful Audiobook Expansions
"Becoming" by Michelle Obama: The audiobook version of Michelle Obama's memoir not only captured traditional readers but also reached a broader audience through its compelling narration by the former First Lady herself. This personal touch added a layer of authenticity that resonated with listeners.

"The Hitchhiker's Guide to the Galaxy" by Douglas Adams: The witty and whimsical nature of this science fiction classic translated seamlessly into the audiobook format. The narration brought out the humor and charm of the story, attracting listeners who might not have picked up the printed version.

Crossing Language Barriers
Audiobooks possess the unique ability to transcend language barriers. Authors can explore translating their works into different languages for audiobook production, opening up their stories to a global audience. This international appeal enhances the book's reach and impact.

The Personal Connection of Author-Narrated Audiobooks
Authors narrating their own audiobooks create a direct and personal connection with listeners. Hearing the nuances of an author's voice adds authenticity and intimacy, fostering a deeper emotional bond between the creator and the audience.

The Sonic Journey of Literature
In the symphony of literary expression, audiobooks play a distinct and harmonious role. They extend the reach of books to individuals who may have otherwise remained untouched by the magic of storytelling. Authors, by embracing the world of audiobooks, not only cater to diverse preferences but also embark on a sonic journey that resonates with a global and varied audience. So, as an

author, consider the power of audiobooks in expanding your horizons and reaching new literary landscapes. Your story deserves to be heard by all ears, not just those leafing through pages.

2
Breaking Barriers

Audiobooks as Catalysts for Literary Accessibility

In the realm of literature, accessibility is a crucial cornerstone that ensures everyone has the opportunity to immerse themselves in the beauty of storytelling. Audiobooks, with their captivating narrations and auditory experiences, stand out as champions in making content accessible to a diverse audience, including those with visual impairments or learning disabilities. In this blog post, we'll explore the profound impact of audiobooks in breaking down barriers and opening the doors of literary enjoyment to a wider and more inclusive audience.

Empowering the Visually Impaired and Beyond
Audiobooks serve as a beacon of literary inclusion for individuals with visual impairments. The power of storytelling comes to life through spoken words, offering a rich and immersive experience that goes beyond the limitations of printed text. For those who cannot rely on visual cues, audiobooks become a gateway to the vast world of literature.

Audiobooks and Learning Disabilities
Beyond visual impairments, audiobooks cater to individuals with various learning disabilities. The auditory nature of these books provides an alternative medium for comprehension, allowing those with reading challenges to engage with content more effectively. This not only fosters a love for literature but also supports educational endeavors by presenting information in a format that suits diverse learning styles.

A Wider Audience, A Richer Tapestry

The beauty of audiobooks lies in their ability to cast a wide net of accessibility, embracing readers of all abilities. By providing an auditory channel for consuming content, audiobooks dismantle barriers that might otherwise hinder individuals from enjoying the wonders of literature. This inclusivity enriches the literary landscape, creating a tapestry woven with the threads of diverse perspectives.

Examples of Audiobook Accessibility Triumphs
"The Harry Potter Series" by J.K. Rowling: Audiobooks narrated by talented individuals, such as Jim Dale and Stephen Fry, made the magical world of Harry Potter accessible to a broader audience, including those with visual impairments. The vivid descriptions and character voices painted a vibrant picture for listeners.

"Educated" by Tara Westover: This memoir, narrated by Julia Whelan, not only captivated traditional readers but also became a beacon of accessibility for those with learning disabilities. The narrative style facilitated a deep understanding of Westover's journey, making the book more inclusive.

Beyond Words: Audiobooks as Learning Tools
Audiobooks are not just a means of entertainment; they serve as valuable learning tools. Educational content, historical accounts, and informative literature become more accessible through the auditory format, catering to a diverse audience with varying learning needs.

The Global Impact of Transcending Language Barriers
Audiobooks, when translated into different languages, contribute to the global accessibility of literature. By breaking language barriers, authors can reach an even broader international audience, ensuring that the universal language of storytelling resonates with people worldwide.

Unveiling the Symphony of Inclusion

In the symphony of literary expression, audiobooks emerge as harmonious instruments that play the tune of inclusion. By making content accessible to those with visual impairments or learning disabilities, audiobooks transform storytelling into a shared experience for everyone. As an author, embracing the audiobook medium not only broadens your readership but also contributes to a more inclusive literary world. So, let the power of audiobooks break down barriers and unveil the symphony of inclusion in the realm of literature.

3
Unleashing the Power of Multitasking

Audiobooks and the Art of Accomplishing More

In a world where time is a precious commodity, the ability to multitask has become a sought-after skill. Audiobooks, with their immersive and portable nature, have seamlessly woven themselves into the fabric of our daily lives. This blog post explores the phenomenon of multitasking convenience through audiobooks, examining how they empower audiences to engage with content in situations where traditional reading might be impractical.

Audiobooks: The Soundtrack of Productivity

In the hustle and bustle of modern life, finding time to sit down with a good book can be a luxury. Audiobooks come to the rescue, transforming mundane activities into opportunities for literary exploration. Whether commuting, exercising, or tackling household chores, multitasking becomes a gateway to a world of stories.

Commuting Adventures with Audiobooks

"The Martian" by Andy Weir: Imagine being stuck in traffic while Mark Watney is stranded on Mars, battling the elements for survival. Audiobooks turn commutes into adventures, allowing listeners to escape the monotony of traffic jams and turn travel time into a literary journey.

"Where the Crawdads Sing" by Delia Owens: A captivating narrative can turn a mundane subway ride into a riveting experience. Audiobooks offer an escape for urban commuters, turning crowded public transportation into a personal reading space.

Exercise Your Body and Mind

Audiobooks and exercise form a dynamic duo, encouraging physical fitness and mental stimulation simultaneously. The rhythmic beats of a morning run or the steady hum of a gym session provide the perfect backdrop for a captivating story.

"Born a Crime" by Trevor Noah: Trevor Noah's memoir is not only a brilliant exploration of his life but also an excellent companion for a jog or workout. The combination of physical activity and engaging storytelling creates a unique synergy that enhances the overall experience.

"The Girl on the Train" by Paula Hawkins: Turn your daily walk into a suspenseful journey with psychological thrillers like "The Girl on the Train." Audiobooks make exercise more enjoyable, encouraging individuals to stay active while getting lost in a good story.

Transforming Chores into Adventures
Household chores often feel like a necessary but mundane part of life. Audiobooks have the power to turn these routine tasks into enjoyable moments of escapism, making the most of every minute spent on domestic responsibilities.

"Harry Potter and the Sorcerer's Stone" by J.K. Rowling: Channel your inner wizard while doing the dishes or folding laundry. The magical world of Harry Potter can make household chores feel like a magical adventure.

"The Joy of Less" by Francine Jay: Minimalism enthusiasts can pair decluttering sessions with audiobooks like "The Joy of Less." The combination of simplifying your space and absorbing valuable insights creates a harmonious experience.

A Symphony of Efficiency and Enjoyment
Audiobooks have redefined the way we engage with literature, seamlessly integrating it into our daily routines. By embracing multitasking convenience, authors and listeners alike participate in a symphony of efficiency and enjoyment. Whether you're

commuting, exercising, or tackling household chores, audiobooks offer a versatile and enriching way to make the most of every moment. So, let the soundtrack of your favorite audiobook accompany you as you navigate the diverse landscapes of your daily life.

4
The Art of Emotion

Audiobooks and the Power of Narration in Creating Heartfelt Connections

In the realm of storytelling, emotions are the threads that weave the tapestry of connection between the audience and the narrative. Audiobooks, with their ability to breathe life into characters through voice inflections and emotions, stand as a testament to the profound impact of narration on the emotional landscape of a story. In this blog post, we explore how the enhanced emotional connection forged by audiobooks deepens the bond between the audience and the narrative.

The Symphony of Narration

Narration in audiobooks is more than just spoken words—it's a performance. A skilled narrator has the power to infuse characters with personality, emotions, and depth, transforming a story into a vivid experience. The emotional nuances conveyed through voice become a bridge, allowing listeners to traverse the emotional terrain of the narrative.

Audiobook Narration: Bringing Characters to Life

"The Great Gatsby" narrated by Jake Gyllenhaal: In this classic, Jake Gyllenhaal's narration adds a layer of sophistication and depth to F. Scott Fitzgerald's characters. The nuances in his voice capture the essence of each persona, intensifying the emotional impact of the narrative.

"The Handmaid's Tale" narrated by Claire Danes: Claire Danes lends her voice to Margaret Atwood's dystopian masterpiece, creating a haunting and emotionally charged atmosphere. Her narration breathes life into the protagonist, Offred, and the emotional struggles she faces.

Emotional Resonance in Characterization
Audiobook narration elevates the emotional resonance of characters, making them more relatable and memorable. The cadence, tone, and emotional intensity conveyed by the narrator add layers to the characters' personalities, forging a deeper connection between the audience and the story.

Immersive Experience: Beyond Words on a Page
The emotional connection facilitated by audiobooks goes beyond the written word on a page. Hearing the laughter, sorrow, or excitement in a narrator's voice immerses listeners in the emotional landscape of the narrative, creating a sensory experience that traditional reading might not fully capture.

Personal Touch: Authors Narrating Their Own Works
"Bossypants" written and narrated by Tina Fey: Tina Fey's narration of her memoir adds a personal touch that resonates with authenticity. Hearing the author's own voice recounting her experiences creates an intimate connection between Fey and the audience.

"Born a Crime" written and narrated by Trevor Noah: Trevor Noah's narration of his memoir brings humor, emotion, and cultural insight to life. His voice becomes a conduit for the emotional journey he shares, fostering a unique bond with the listeners.

A Journey of Shared Emotions
Audiobooks become a shared emotional journey between the narrator and the audience. The laughter, tears, and moments of suspense are not just words on a page but a collaborative experience where the narrator and listener embark on a joint exploration of the story's emotional landscape.

Where Voices Echo in Hearts

In the world of audiobooks, voices echo in the hearts of listeners, creating a symphony of emotions that lingers long after the narrative concludes. The enhanced emotional connection forged through narration is a testament to the transformative power of storytelling. Authors and narrators alike have the ability to cultivate a profound bond with their audience, one that transcends the boundaries of written words. So, whether you're a creator or a listener, let the voices in audiobooks resonate in your heart, forging connections that endure beyond the final chapter.

5
Beyond Borders

Audiobooks and the Global Tapestry of Storytelling

In the digital age, the world is more connected than ever before, and the realm of literature is no exception. Audiobooks, with their unique ability to transcend language barriers, have emerged as global ambassadors of storytelling. This blog post explores how audiobooks, through translation into different languages, offer authors a passport to a broader international market, fostering a truly global appeal.

The Universal Language of Audiobooks
In a world where languages are diverse and varied, audiobooks become a bridge that unites listeners from different corners of the globe. The spoken word, accompanied by the nuances of narration, has the power to resonate across cultures, creating a shared experience that transcends linguistic boundaries.

Audiobooks in Translation: Opening New Horizons
"The Alchemist" by Paulo Coelho: Originally written in Portuguese, "The Alchemist" has been translated into numerous languages for its audiobook versions. This global accessibility has allowed the profound wisdom of Coelho's work to reach audiences worldwide, fostering a universal connection.

"The Girl with the Dragon Tattoo" by Stieg Larsson: This Swedish thriller, translated into English and various other languages for its audiobook editions, showcases how translation expands the reach of a gripping narrative. The intense storytelling becomes a global phenomenon accessible to a diverse audience.

Breaking Down Language Barriers

Audiobooks play a pivotal role in breaking down language barriers that might impede the reach of written works. Through translation, authors can share their stories with individuals who may not have access to the original language, creating a more inclusive and diverse readership.

Multilingual Narration: A Symphony of Voices
"One Hundred Years of Solitude" by Gabriel García Márquez: This masterpiece has been translated into various languages for its audiobook editions, featuring narrators who capture the essence of Márquez's magical realism. The multilingual narration enhances the global appeal of this literary classic.

"The Three-Body Problem" by Liu Cixin: Originally in Chinese, this sci-fi novel's audiobook versions have been translated into English, allowing the work of Liu Cixin to reach an international audience. The diverse narrators contribute to the global resonance of the story.

Cultural Exchange Through Audiobooks
Audiobooks, translated and narrated in different languages, become agents of cultural exchange. Listeners gain insights into diverse perspectives, traditions, and storytelling styles, fostering a rich tapestry of global literary experiences.

Accessibility Across Borders
"The Diary of a Young Girl" by Anne Frank: Translated into numerous languages for audiobook adaptations, Anne Frank's diary provides a poignant example of how translation enhances accessibility. The emotional impact of Anne's words transcends borders, resonating with listeners worldwide.

"The Shadow of the Wind" by Carlos Ruiz Zafón: Originally in Spanish, this novel's audiobook versions have been translated into English and other languages. The translation ensures that Zafón's intricate storytelling is accessible to a diverse global audience.

A Worldwide Symphony of Stories

In the global orchestra of storytelling, audiobooks serve as instruments that harmonize across languages and cultures. The ability to translate books into different languages for audiobooks opens new chapters for authors, inviting a global audience to partake in the beauty of diverse narratives. So, whether you're an author seeking to reach new horizons or a listener eager to explore tales from around the world, let audiobooks be the vessels that carry stories across borders, creating a worldwide symphony of shared experiences.

6
A Voice Beyond Words

The Intimate Connection of Author-Narrated Audiobooks

In the ever-evolving landscape of storytelling, authors are discovering new ways to forge intimate connections with their readers. One such avenue is through the medium of audiobooks, where authors take on the role of narrator, infusing their words with a personal touch that transcends the written page. This blog post explores the profound impact of an author's personal narration on audiobooks, creating a unique and direct connection between the creator and the audience.

The Art of Narration: Beyond the Written Word

Narrating one's own audiobook is an art form that goes beyond the act of writing. Authors, by lending their voices to their stories, offer listeners a more immersive and personal experience. The intonation, nuances, and emotional depth conveyed in the author's voice become an extension of the narrative itself.

Embracing Authenticity

"Becoming" by Michelle Obama: In her memoir, Michelle Obama narrates the audiobook, allowing listeners to hear her story in her own words and voice. The personal touch adds authenticity, providing an intimate journey into the life of the former First Lady.

"Born a Crime" by Trevor Noah: Trevor Noah's narration of his memoir brings humor, cultural insights, and a personal touch that resonates with listeners. The author's voice becomes a vehicle for conveying the emotional and humorous nuances of his experiences.

Direct Connection with the Author

Author-narrated audiobooks offer a direct line of connection between the creator and the audience. Listeners feel as if they are personally being guided through the narrative by the individual who conceived the story, adding a layer of intimacy to the entire experience.

Shared Emotions and Insights
"Bossypants" written and narrated by Tina Fey: Tina Fey's narration of her comedic memoir brings her wit and humor to life in a way that only she can. Listeners share in the laughter and insights as if they are sitting across from the author, engaging in a one-on-one conversation.

"The Long Hard Road Out of Hell" by Marilyn Manson and Neil Strauss: Co-authored and narrated by Marilyn Manson, this audiobook allows listeners to delve into the artist's mind and experiences in a uniquely personal way. Manson's narration adds depth to the storytelling, creating an immersive journey.

Capturing the Essence of Characters
Authors, being intimately familiar with their characters, can capture their essence in ways that resonate authentically. The inflections, tones, and expressions in the author's voice become a vehicle for conveying the intricacies of each character's personality.

Unveiling Layers of Intimacy
"Kitchen Confidential" by Anthony Bourdain: Bourdain's narration of his culinary memoir creates an intimate atmosphere as he shares personal anecdotes and reflections. The author's voice becomes a companion, revealing layers of his personality that go beyond the written words.

"The Glass Castle" by Jeannette Walls: Walls narrates her memoir, providing a raw and honest account of her unconventional upbringing. The author's personal touch in narration unveils the emotional layers of the story, creating a powerful and intimate connection with the audience.

A Conversation Across Time and Space

Author-narrated audiobooks transcend the boundaries of traditional storytelling. They become more than a medium for conveying a narrative—they transform into a conversation between the author and the listener. As an author, embracing the opportunity to narrate your own audiobook adds a personal touch that echoes across time and space, creating an enduring and intimate connection with your audience. So, whether you're a writer or a listener, let the author's voice be the bridge that invites you into the heart of a story, forging a connection that lingers long after the final chapter.

7
Sonic Versatility

The All-Encompassing World of Audiobooks Across Genres

In the symphony of literary expression, audiobooks emerge as versatile instruments capable of playing diverse tunes across various genres. From the realms of fiction to the corridors of self-help, audiobooks offer an immersive experience that resonates with a broad spectrum of audiences. This blog post delves into the adaptability of audiobooks for different genres, illustrating how this medium seamlessly integrates into the fabric of storytelling, attracting a diverse and eager audience.

Audiobooks as Chameleons of Literature

Audiobooks are not bound by the constraints of a specific genre; instead, they serve as chameleons, adapting to the nuances and tones of various literary landscapes. Whether it's the suspenseful atmosphere of a thriller or the introspective journey of a self-help guide, audiobooks mold themselves to the essence of the story, creating a dynamic and engaging experience.

The Global Phenomenon of Fiction Audiobooks

"The Da Vinci Code" by Dan Brown: This gripping thriller comes alive in its audiobook adaptation, with the narrator skillfully navigating through the twists and turns of the plot. The suspenseful ambiance is heightened, providing listeners with an immersive experience.

"Circe" by Madeline Miller: In the realm of mythology and fantasy, "Circe" captivates listeners with its rich narrative and mythical world. The audiobook, narrated by Perdita Weeks, adds a layer of enchantment, making the ancient tale accessible to a modern audience.

Navigating Emotional Landscapes in Non-Fiction
Audiobooks are not confined to the realms of fiction alone; they extend their reach into the world of non-fiction, navigating the emotional landscapes of self-help, memoirs, and educational content.

The Guiding Voice in Self-Help
"Atomic Habits" by James Clear: James Clear's guide to forming positive habits is brought to life in its audiobook version. Clear's own narration adds a personal touch, making the principles of habit formation more accessible and relatable to listeners.

"Educated" by Tara Westover: The powerful memoir of Tara Westover is amplified in its audiobook, narrated by Julia Whelan. The emotional journey of self-discovery and resilience is conveyed with a depth that enhances the impact of Westover's narrative.

Children's Literature in the Audiobook Realm
Audiobooks extend their adaptability even to children's literature, turning storytelling into an auditory adventure for young listeners.

The Magical Narration for Young Audiences
"Harry Potter" series by J.K. Rowling: The magic of Hogwarts comes to life in the audiobook versions of the beloved series. Narrated by Jim Dale and Stephen Fry, the audiobooks transport young audiences into the enchanting world of wizardry with captivating narration.

"The Chronicles of Narnia" by C.S. Lewis: This timeless classic is reborn through audiobooks, with narrators like Kenneth Branagh and Michael York adding a magical touch to the adventures of Lucy, Edmund, and the mystical land of Narnia.

The Educational Landscape of Audiobooks
Audiobooks extend their adaptability even into the educational realm, providing a unique platform for learning and exploration.

Narrating Knowledge

"Sapiens: A Brief History of Humankind" by Yuval Noah Harari: Harari's exploration of human history is made accessible through audiobooks, allowing listeners to engage with complex concepts narrated in a compelling and digestible manner.

"The Subtle Art of Not Giving a F*ck" by Mark Manson: This self-help classic transforms into an engaging experience in its audiobook form, with Manson's narration infusing the content with his unique voice and perspective.

The Universal Symphony of Audiobooks

Audiobooks, with their adaptability for different genres, create a universal symphony that resonates with readers and listeners across diverse literary tastes. Whether you're a fan of fiction, non-fiction, or children's literature, the immersive experience offered by audiobooks transcends genre boundaries. As an author, embracing the audiobook medium opens the door to a vast and diverse audience, allowing your story to find resonance in the ears of listeners eager for a unique auditory journey. So, let your narrative be the melody that plays across genres, captivating audiences and enriching the world of literature through the versatile magic of audiobooks.

8
Sound Investments

The Profitable Symphony of Audiobooks in Authorship

In the dynamic landscape of publishing, authors are navigating new avenues to not only share their stories but also to explore the realms of profitability. Audiobooks, emerging as a powerful and lucrative market, offer authors the opportunity to enhance their earnings through royalties. This blog post delves into the financial benefits of audiobooks, showcasing how this growing market can be a sound and profitable addition to an author's overall book sales strategy.

The Rising Crescendo of Audiobook Profitability
Audiobooks are not merely a trend; they represent a growing market that continues to gain traction among readers and listeners alike. The demand for audiobooks has created a robust ecosystem where authors can reap financial rewards through royalties, making it a compelling avenue for maximizing profits.

The Royalty Symphony: Earning from Audiobook Sales
Audible's Royalty Share Program: Platforms like Audible offer authors the opportunity to earn royalties through their Royalty Share program. Authors can opt to share royalties with their audiobook narrators, providing a collaborative and profitable incentive for both parties.

ACX (Audiobook Creation Exchange): ACX, an Amazon company, provides authors with a platform to produce and distribute their audiobooks. Through royalty-sharing models, authors can earn a percentage of sales for each audiobook sold, contributing to the overall profitability of their literary endeavors.

Diversifying Revenue Streams
Audiobooks, as a profitable addition to an author's strategy, contribute to the diversification of revenue streams. In a landscape where readers consume content through various mediums, audiobooks offer an additional avenue for authors to generate income beyond traditional print and e-book sales.

The Global Reach of Audiobook Sales
"The Silent Patient" by Alex Michaelides: This psychological thriller became a bestseller in audiobook format, showcasing the global appeal of the medium. The author, by tapping into the audiobook market, expanded the reach of the story and increased the overall profitability of the book.

"Becoming" by Michelle Obama: Michelle Obama's memoir not only achieved tremendous success in print but also became a hit in audiobook form. The audiobook's profitability contributed to the overall success of the book, reaching audiences around the world.

Leveraging Audiobooks for Brand Building
Audiobooks offer authors a unique opportunity to strengthen their brand and enhance their visibility in the literary world. The profitability derived from audiobook sales goes beyond immediate financial gains, contributing to the author's overall brand building and market presence.

The Audiobook Advantage in Today's Market
"Educated" by Tara Westover: The success of Tara Westover's memoir in audiobook format highlights the advantage of leveraging audiobooks in today's market. The profitability of the audiobook version adds a layer of financial success to the overall impact of the book.

"The Subtle Art of Not Giving a F*ck" by Mark Manson: This self-help classic's profitability in audiobook sales showcases the potential for authors in genres beyond fiction. The financial returns contribute to the author's brand recognition and standing in the literary world.

Orchestrating Success with Audiobooks

As authors navigate the diverse landscape of publishing, the profitability of audiobooks shines as a beacon of opportunity. The growing market, coupled with the potential for earning royalties, makes audiobooks a lucrative addition to an author's overall book sales strategy. Beyond the financial gains, audiobooks contribute to brand building, global reach, and the creation of a dynamic and diversified revenue stream. So, whether you're a seasoned author or an aspiring writer, consider the symphony of possibilities that audiobooks bring to your literary journey—a harmonious blend of storytelling and profitability that resonates with readers and listeners worldwide.

9
Riding the Sonic Wave

Authors Embracing the Audiobook Revolution

In the ever-evolving landscape of literature, authors are navigating the tides of technological trends that shape the way stories are consumed. Audiobooks, propelled by the rise of platforms like Audible, have surged in popularity, creating a sonic revolution in the literary world. This blog post explores the importance of authors embracing technological trends, particularly the audiobook wave, to stay relevant in the modern literary landscape.

The Audiobook Renaissance: A Sonic Revolution
As technology continues to weave its intricate tapestry into every aspect of our lives, literature undergoes a transformation of its own. Audiobooks, once a niche market, have experienced a renaissance, becoming a mainstream phenomenon fueled by the accessibility and convenience offered by platforms like Audible.

Audible: The Sonic Hub of Audiobook Evolution
Audible Originals: Audible, a leading audiobook platform, has not only facilitated the distribution of audiobooks but has also given rise to Audible Originals. These exclusive audiobook productions showcase the platform's commitment to pushing the boundaries of storytelling through technology.

Subscription Models: Audible's subscription models provide users with a seamless and cost-effective way to consume audiobooks. Authors who embrace this technological trend tap into a subscription-based economy, ensuring a steady stream of revenue as their audiobooks reach a wider audience.

Staying Relevant in the Sonic Landscape

Authors, by embracing the audiobook revolution, position themselves at the forefront of literary trends. Staying relevant in the modern literary landscape involves recognizing the shifting preferences of readers and listeners and adapting to the technological tools that cater to those preferences.

Relevance Through Adaptation
"The Martian" by Andy Weir: The success of "The Martian" in both print and audiobook formats illustrates how an author can leverage technological trends to stay relevant. The audiobook's popularity, with its immersive narration, contributed to the overall success of the story.

"Dune" by Frank Herbert: A science fiction classic like "Dune" remains relevant through audiobook adaptations, capturing the attention of modern listeners who prefer the convenience of audio storytelling. Authors of timeless works can extend their reach by embracing audiobook technology.

Accessibility and Convenience for the Modern Reader
The modern reader, often juggling a myriad of responsibilities, gravitates towards convenience and accessibility. Audiobooks, available at the touch of a button on smartphones and other devices, provide a solution that aligns with the fast-paced, multitasking lifestyle of contemporary audiences.

Convenience in the Commute
"Where the Crawdads Sing" by Delia Owens: Commuters can seamlessly integrate audiobooks into their daily routines, turning traffic jams or public transportation into opportunities for literary exploration. "Where the Crawdads Sing" gained popularity not only in print but also as an audiobook, catering to on-the-go readers.

"The Girl on the Train" by Paula Hawkins: The audiobook adaptation of this psychological thriller offers a convenient option for those who prefer to engage with gripping narratives during their commutes. Authors who recognize and leverage this trend position themselves as accessible to a broader audience.

Future-Proofing Literary Careers

Embracing technological trends, especially those related to audiobooks, is a form of future-proofing for authors. As the digital landscape continues to evolve, staying ahead of the curve ensures that authors can navigate the changing currents of reader preferences and technological advancements.

The Resonance of Modern Storytelling

"The Silent Patient" by Alex Michaelides: The success of this psychological thriller in audiobook form underscores the resonance of modern storytelling. Authors who adapt their works to audiobooks tap into the preferences of a tech-savvy audience seeking immersive and convenient literary experiences.

"Atomic Habits" by James Clear: In the realm of self-help, "Atomic Habits" maintains relevance by embracing the audiobook trend. The author's insights, delivered through narration, connect with listeners seeking personal development in a format that aligns with modern lifestyles.

A Sonic Symphony of Literary Evolution

As authors embark on the journey of literary creation, embracing technological trends becomes a strategic imperative. The audiobook revolution, fueled by platforms like Audible, represents a sonic symphony of literary evolution. Authors who recognize the significance of this trend position themselves not only at the forefront of modern storytelling but also in the hearts and ears of a diverse and tech-savvy audience. So, let the words echo in the digital realm, and authors, ride the sonic wave of audiobook popularity to stay relevant in the ever-evolving landscape of literature.

10
Amplifying Your Narrative

The Marketing Power of Audiobooks

In the dynamic realm of publishing, authors are discovering that audiobooks are not just a medium for storytelling; they are potent tools for marketing and exposure. The production of an audiobook extends beyond the act of narrating words—it becomes a strategic move to garner attention, create buzz, and open doors to promotional opportunities. This blog post explores how producing an audiobook can serve as a powerful marketing tool, amplifying your narrative and expanding your reach in the literary landscape.

Audiobooks as Catalysts for Buzz and Attention
Audiobooks have emerged as more than a format for literary consumption; they are agents of buzz and attention. The unique appeal of audiobooks attracts a diverse audience, and the process of creating one can generate excitement around your book.

Buzzworthy Audiobook Examples
"The Hitchhiker's Guide to the Galaxy" by Douglas Adams: The audiobook adaptation of this classic science fiction novel not only preserves the humor and wit of the original but also generates buzz among fans. The engaging narration by Stephen Fry adds an extra layer of enjoyment, creating anticipation and conversation.

"Daisy Jones & The Six" by Taylor Jenkins Reid: This novel, presented in an oral history format, translates seamlessly into an audiobook. The captivating performances by a full cast contribute to the buzz surrounding the story, making it a standout example of how audiobooks can elevate the narrative and generate interest.

Audiobooks as Gateways to Promotional Activities

Producing an audiobook opens the door to a realm of promotional activities within the audiobook space. It becomes a catalyst for interviews, podcast features, and collaborations that can further amplify your book's visibility.

Interviews and Author Spotlights
Author Interviews on Audiobook Platforms: Platforms like Audible often feature author interviews and behind-the-scenes content, providing authors with an opportunity to connect with their audience. This additional content becomes a promotional asset, driving interest in the audiobook and the author.

Audiobook Narrator Collaborations: Collaborating with audiobook narrators for promotional activities, such as joint interviews or social media campaigns, can leverage their fan base and extend the reach of your book. The partnership becomes a mutually beneficial promotional endeavor.

Podcast Features and Audiobook Excerpts
Podcast Features on Audiobook Themes: Appearing on podcasts that focus on audiobooks, literature, or storytelling allows authors to share insights about the audiobook creation process. These features not only promote the audiobook but also provide valuable content for engaged listeners.

Audiobook Excerpt Teasers on Podcasts: Teasing audiobook excerpts on relevant podcasts creates anticipation and curiosity among potential listeners. It serves as a sneak peek into the immersive experience offered by the audiobook, enticing audiences to explore the full narrative.

Leveraging Social Media and Audiobook Trailers
Audiobook Trailers on Social Media Platforms: Creating engaging audiobook trailers and sharing them across social media platforms can captivate audiences visually. These trailers serve as compelling marketing tools, offering a glimpse into the auditory journey that awaits listeners.

Author Read-Aloud Sessions: Sharing snippets of authors reading excerpts from their audiobooks in video format adds a personal touch to promotional efforts. Social media platforms become stages for connecting with readers and generating excitement about the audiobook.

Building Community and Fostering Engagement
Audiobooks, as marketing tools, contribute to building a community around your book. The immersive nature of audio storytelling fosters engagement, creating a loyal audience that eagerly anticipates future releases and promotional activities.

Virtual Book Clubs and Audiobook Discussions
Online Book Club Events: Hosting virtual book club events focused on the audiobook version can foster community engagement. Discussions around the narrative, characters, and the audiobook production process contribute to a vibrant and interactive literary community.

Exclusive Audiobook Content for Subscribers: Providing exclusive audiobook content, such as bonus chapters or author commentary, to subscribers builds a dedicated community. This strategy not only rewards loyal readers but also serves as a unique marketing approach.

Amplifying Your Story, Expanding Your Reach
In the symphony of book marketing, audiobooks play a pivotal role as instruments of amplification. Beyond their immersive storytelling capabilities, audiobooks serve as catalysts for buzz, attention, and promotional activities within the audiobook space. Authors who recognize the marketing power of audiobooks position themselves to reach broader audiences, connect with readers in new ways, and create a lasting impact in the literary landscape. So, let the narrative unfold in the auditory realm, and may your audiobook be the crescendo that resonates far and wide, amplifying your story and expanding your reach in the dynamic world of literature.

About the Author

B Alan Bourgeois began his writing career at the age of 12, writing screenplays for the Adam-12 show. Despite not submitting them for review, this experience sparked his passion for writing. However, he followed the advice of his generation and pursued higher education to secure a stable job. It wasn't until 1989, after taking a writing class at a community college, that Bourgeois wrote a short story that was published. Since then, he has written over 48 short stories and published more than 10 books, including the award-winning spiritual thriller "Extinguishing the Light."

Bourgeois has become a champion for authors and founded the Texas Authors Association in 2011 to help Texas authors better market and sell their books. This led to the creation of the Texas Authors Institute of History, Inc., and the first online museum of its kind, the Texas Authors Institute. He also created several short story contests and fundraising programs for Texas students and consolidated small-town book festivals into the Lone Star Festival, promoting Texas authors, musicians, artists, and filmmakers. In 2016, he founded the Authors Marketing Event and added a Certification program in 2017, allowing attendees to gain accreditation for their hard work in learning book marketing. His recent focus has been on assisting authors of all levels to become successful Authorpreneurs through the Authors School of Business, which offers programs to help grow their careers. He is currently working with NFTs for authors to help them increase their income channels.

Top Ten Book Series and Other Books by the Author

Available at Your Favorite Bookstore

100+ Questions a Writer/Author Should Ask

Looking to take your writing career to the next level? Look no further than "100+ Questions a Writer/Author Should Ask"! With over 100 questions curated by Award-Winning Author and speaker B Alan Bourgeois, the founder and CEO of the Authors School of Business, this book is a must-have for any aspiring or established writer. Bourgeois, a seasoned publisher, author advocate, and educator brings his wealth of experience to the table to help you better understand the publishing world and succeed in your career. Don't miss out on this valuable resource.

Top Ten Mistakes Authors Make when Creating a Book Cover

Your book cover is your first impression. Don't let a lackluster design hold you back. "Top Ten Mistakes Authors Make When Creating a Book Cover" is your comprehensive guide to avoiding common pitfalls and creating a cover that truly represents your work. Discover practical tips on how to choose the right colors, fonts, and design, and avoid using low-quality images and cluttered layouts. With real-world examples and expert advice, this book will help you create a cover that grabs readers' attention and leads to more sales.

Don't let a poorly designed book cover hold you back from success. Whether you're self-publishing or working with a traditional publisher, "Top Ten Mistakes Authors Make When Creating a Book Cover" is a must-read. Order your copy today and take your book to the next level!

Top Ten Things to Consider for a Great Sales Pitch

Are you struggling to create a sales pitch that resonates with your audience? Look no further than "Top Ten Things to Consider for a Great Sales Pitch"! This ultimate guide will take you through the ten most important steps to creating a sales pitch that will grab your target audience's attention and convince them to buy your book.

Learn how to identify your target audience and highlight the unique value of your book, using emotional language to connect with readers on a personal level. Be concise and to the point, and practice your pitch until you can deliver it smoothly and confidently. Incorporate social proof and visuals to make your pitch more compelling, and tailor it to the specific interests and needs of your audience.

Above all, be authentic and genuine. With the help of "Top Ten Things to Consider for a Great Sales Pitch", you'll be able to create a sales pitch that not only sells your book but also connects with your audience and builds a loyal fan base. Don't miss out on this essential resource for any author looking to take their sales pitch to the next level!

Top Ten Publishing Issues Authors Deal With

Are you an aspiring author struggling with the daunting publishing process? Look no further than "Top Ten Publishing Issues Authors Deal With." This essential guide tackles the most common challenges writers face, including rejection, editing, marketing, distribution, audience building, time management, and legal issues like copyright infringement. Our expert advice will help you navigate the complex world of publishing and achieve success. Plus, we'll guide you through the formatting process, even for ebooks that need to work on multiple devices and software. Don't let self-doubt and imposter syndrome hinder your progress - get the knowledge you need to thrive in the publishing world. Order your copy of "Top Ten Publishing Issues Authors Deal With" today.

Top Ten Marketing Materials an Author Should Use

"Top Ten Marketing Items Authors Should Use" is the ultimate guide for authors who want to boost book sales and increase visibility. Discover the top ten marketing materials every author should use, including eye-catching bookmarks, business cards, posters, and book trailers. You'll also learn insider tips on how to write an attention-grabbing press release and build an author website that attracts readers and media attention. Plus, social media marketing, author blogging, email newsletters, and swag creation strategies will help you connect with readers, build your author brand, and create a loyal fan base. Don't let your book languish in obscurity - get your copy of "Top Ten Marketing Items Authors Should Use" today and take the first step toward successful book promotion!

Top Ten Mistakes an Author Makes Marketing Their Books

Are you an author struggling to make a name for yourself in the crowded world of book marketing? Do you want to avoid the most common mistakes that authors make when promoting their books? Then look no further than "Top 10 Mistakes Authors Make Marketing Their Books" by B Alan Bourgeois.

As an award-winning author and author advocate with years of experience in the publishing industry, Bourgeois has seen it all when it comes to book marketing. In this insightful guide, he shares the top 10 mistakes that authors make and provides practical advice on how to avoid them.
Whether you're a first-time author or a seasoned pro, "Top 10 Mistakes Authors Make Marketing Their Books" is the essential guide for taking your book marketing to the next level. With Bourgeois's expert guidance, you'll learn how to identify your target audience, build a strong online presence, engage with readers, and leverage book reviews to increase sales.

Don't let common marketing mistakes hold you back from the success you deserve. Get your copy of "Top 10 Mistakes Authors Make Marketing Their Books" today and start marketing your book like a pro!

Top Ten Mistakes Authors Make During an Interview

Are you tired of stumbling through interviews, leaving the audience uninterested and disengaged? Do you struggle with staying focused and concise when answering tough questions? Look no further!

Our book provides you with the top ten mistakes authors commonly make at interviews and gives you practical tips on how to avoid them. From preparing adequately by researching the interviewer and their audience, to staying authentic and avoiding complex jargon, we cover it all.

Don't let your lack of enthusiasm or defensiveness turn off your audience. Instead, learn how to show genuine interest in your topic and stay calm during challenging questions. And most importantly, don't forget to thank your interviewer and audience for their time and attention - it can make all the difference in leaving a positive impression.

So, are you ready to improve your interview skills and leave a lasting impact on your audience? Get your copy of "Top Ten Mistakes Authors Do at Interviews" today!

Top Ten Mistakes Authors Make Presenting at Events

Are you an author struggling to present at events? "Top Ten Mistakes Authors Make Presenting at Events" is here to help you avoid common pitfalls and present your best self. Learn how to tailor your presentation to the audience's needs, engage with them effectively, promote your book without being pushy, and more!

With this ultimate guide, you'll avoid going off-topic, losing your audience's attention, and being dull and uninteresting. Practice and rehearse your presentation to deliver it smoothly and confidently. Get your copy of "Top Ten Mistakes Authors Make Presenting at Events" today and make the most of every event you attend!

Top Ten AI Programs Apps Authors Should Use

Attention all writers and authors! Are you looking for ways to improve your writing, stay organized, and streamline your workflow? Look no further than our latest book "Top Ten AI Programs/Apps a Writer/Author Should Use". In this book, we have compiled a list of the top ten AI programs and apps that will help you with your writing, marketing, and workflow. From Grammarly and ProWritingAid to Hemingway and Dragon Dictation, these programs will help you write a great book.

Although the author has not used all of the programs listed, this list was compiled in 2023 from various sources and provides valuable insight into the most effective AI tools for writers and authors. Keep in mind that the AI community is constantly developing new resources and programs, so this list may not be the most up-to-date.

Don't miss out on the opportunity to improve your writing and streamline your workflow. Order "Top Ten AI programs/Apps a writer/author should use" now and start using these powerful tools to produce your best work.

Top Ten Advantages Indie Authors Have Over Traditional Authors

"Top Ten Advantages Indie Authors Have over Traditional" is the ultimate guide for authors looking to take control of their publishing process. With complete control over everything from writing to distribution, independent authors have more flexibility and creative control over their work.

This book highlights the benefits of indie publishing, including higher royalties, faster publishing timelines, the ability to target niche markets, and global distribution through online retailers. If you want more control over your book's content and the ability to reach readers worldwide, "Top Ten Advantages Indie Authors Have over Traditional" is a must-read. Get your copy today and start your journey towards independent publishing success!

Top Ten Pieces of Advice from an Author Advocate & Consultant

"Top Ten Pieces of Advice from an Author Advocate & Consultant" is the ultimate guide for aspiring writers. Learn from an experienced author consultant and advocate and take your writing career to the next level. From building an author platform to developing a marketing plan, this book offers invaluable insights and practical tips to help you achieve your writing goals and make your work stand out. Start your journey to becoming a successful author today by purchasing this must-have resource.

Top Twelve Things to Make the Year of the Indie Authors Great

Are you an indie author looking to make 2024 a great year for your writing career? Then look no further than the book "Top Twelve Things to Make the Year of the Indie Authors Great." This book offers valuable insights into the top 12 things that could make 2024 a great year for indie authors to gain more readers.

With increased acceptance of self-publishing and better distribution channels, indie authors have more options than ever before to reach a wider audience. Additionally, the rise of social media platforms and digital marketing offers affordable ways for authors to connect with readers and promote their work.

But that's not all. The book also covers the importance of collaborating with other authors, the increasing popularity of audiobooks, and the need for more diverse representation in literature. For those looking to improve their writing skills and production quality, the book offers insights into the better tools and resources available to indie authors.

Finally, the book covers opportunities for indie authors to engage with their readers, showcase their work at book festivals and online events, and collaborate with traditional publishers. In short, "Top Twelve Things to Make the Year of the Indie Authors Great" is a must-read for any indie author looking to take their writing career to the next level in 2024.

Top Ten Steps for a Writers Self-Care

Writing can be an exciting and fulfilling pursuit, but it can also be stressful and overwhelming. As an author, it's important to prioritize your mental and physical health to avoid burnout and ensure longevity in your career. The Writer's Self-Care Handbook provides a comprehensive guide to help you balance your work and personal life, manage stress, and prioritize your well-being.

In this book, you'll discover practical tips and strategies for taking breaks, practicing mindfulness, setting boundaries, staying organized, connecting with others, taking care of your physical health, practicing self-compassion, finding healthy ways to manage stress, taking time for hobbies, and seeking support when needed. Whether you're a seasoned author or just starting, The Writer's Self-Care Handbook offers valuable insights and advice to help you thrive in your writing career while taking care of yourself. Take the first step towards a healthier, happier writing life by getting your copy today!

Top Ten Steps to Finding the Right Editor

Are you struggling to find the right editor for your writing project? Look no further than "The Author's Guide to Finding and Working with the Right Editor." In this comprehensive guide, we provide the top ten things authors should keep in mind when finding and working with an editor. From determining your editing needs to maintaining a positive relationship with your editor, this guide covers everything you need to know to ensure a successful collaboration. Learn how to research potential editors, check their credentials, communicate, be open to feedback, and more. Whether you're a first-time author or a seasoned pro, this guide is essential for anyone looking to take their writing to the next level with the help of a skilled and trusted editor.

Top Ten Ways to Brand Yourself as an Author

As an author, it's not just enough to write an amazing book. In today's crowded marketplace, building a brand is essential to stand out and make a lasting impression on readers. In "Brand Yourself as an Author," we provide a top ten guide to help you define your brand identity, create a unique logo, develop a consistent visual identity, build a professional website, use social media to promote your brand, create valuable content, leverage email marketing, collaborate with other authors and brands, participate in events and conferences, and stay true to your brand. With our actionable tips, you'll learn how to build a strong and recognizable brand that resonates with your audience and sets you apart in the competitive world of publishing. Don't miss out on this essential guide to building your author brand!

Top Ten Keys for Successful Writing and Productivity

Are you an aspiring writer struggling to make writing a regular habit? Do you need help setting realistic goals and managing your time effectively to achieve success as an author? Look no further than "The Successful Author's Guide to Writing and Productivity." This comprehensive guide offers practical tips on making writing a habit, setting achievable goals, managing your time, focusing on quality, editing and revising, seeking feedback, building an audience, networking, staying organized, and staying motivated. With advice from successful authors, editors, and writing coaches, this book is a must-have for anyone looking to achieve success as an author. Whether you're a new writer or an experienced author looking to take your writing to the next level, "The Successful Author's Guide to Writing and Productivity" will provide you with the tools and techniques you need to achieve your writing goals. Don't wait any longer to become the successful author you've always wanted to be - grab a copy of "The Successful Author's Guide to Writing and Productivity" today!

Top Ten Keys to the Business of Writing

Are you an aspiring or established author struggling with the business side of publishing? Look no further than The Business of Writing: A Comprehensive Guide for Authors. This essential guide provides in-depth information on the top ten items that every author needs to understand, from publishing contracts to managing finances. Learn how to negotiate contract terms, calculate royalties, promote and market your book, build an author platform, and understand copyright laws and intellectual property. You'll also gain insights into the publishing industry, professional networking, and ongoing professional development. With practical advice and expert insights, The Business of Writing is the ultimate resource for authors who want to succeed in the competitive world of publishing.

Top Ten Steps to Research Like a Pro

Writing a book can be a daunting task, but researching to support your writing can be just as challenging. With "Research Like a Pro: The Ultimate Guide for Writers," you'll learn how to conduct research like a pro, from identifying your research needs to analyzing your findings.

This book provides practical tips on how to use reliable sources, develop a research plan, and organize your materials effectively. You'll learn how to take detailed notes, keep track of citations, and analyze your research to identify patterns and themes.

With "Research Like a Pro," you'll be equipped with the knowledge and tools to effectively use research to support your writing. Whether you're a new writer or a seasoned pro, this book will help you take your research skills to the next level and produce high-quality writing that is well-supported and grounded in evidence.

Top Ten Steps to Market Mastery for Authors

Introducing "Top Ten Steps to Market Mastery for Authors." This comprehensive guide is the key to successfully publishing your book and achieving commercial success. It goes beyond simply writing a book and equips you with the essential knowledge and tools to understand and captivate your target market.

From conducting thorough market research to analyzing sales data, "Market Mastery" covers it all. Discover how to leverage social media effectively, connect with readers at book fairs and conferences, and gain valuable insights through writing groups. Stay ahead of industry trends and developments to keep your book relevant and appealing to your audience.

No matter if you're a first-time author or a seasoned pro, "Market Mastery" will empower you to identify your target audience, understand their preferences, and distinguish your book from competitors. With a strategic marketing approach and willingness to adapt, you'll be on the path to commercial success. Get ready to conquer your target audience and take your writing career to new heights with "Market Mastery."

Top Ten Steps to Creating an Author Platform

Are you an author looking to build your online presence and connect with your readership? Then " Top Ten Steps to Creating an Author Platform " is the perfect resource for you. With practical tips on defining your target audience, establishing a website, creating a blog, building an email list, utilizing social media, attending events and conferences, collaborating with other authors, offering free content, and being consistent, this guide has everything you need to build and maintain a strong author platform. By following the advice of successful authors and marketing experts, you'll learn how to attract readers, establish yourself as an authority in your field, and promote your work effectively. Whether you're a new or experienced author, " Top Ten Steps to Creating an Author Platform " is an essential tool for any writer looking to take their career to the next level. Don't wait any longer to build your online presence - grab a copy today and start building your author platform!

Top Ten Keys to Author Networking

Are you an aspiring author struggling to make industry connections? Are you looking for ways to expand your network and take your writing career to the next level? Look no further than " Top Ten Keys to Author Networking." This comprehensive guide offers practical advice on attending conferences and events, joining writing organizations, connecting on social media, attending book signings and readings, participating in online forums, attending book fairs, joining Twitter pitch parties, reaching out to authors in your genre, and maintaining a professional and polite demeanor. With tips from successful authors and industry professionals, this book is a must-have for any writer looking to make meaningful connections in the publishing world. Don't miss out on the opportunity to expand your network and increase your chances of success - grab a copy of " Top Ten Keys to Author Networking " today!

Top Ten Reasons an Author Should Use NFT and Blockchain

Top Ten Reasons an Author Should Use NFT and Blockchain is packed with invaluable insights and practical advice, this ultimate guide empowers authors on their journey to digital publishing success. Discover compelling reasons to embrace NFTs, from ensuring authenticity and automating royalties to exploring limited editions and global accessibility. Gain essential knowledge on creating NFTs, mastering smart contracts, and navigating legal considerations. Don't miss your chance to create a lasting legacy and tap into the transformative power of NFTs and blockchain. Get your copy today and embark on a journey towards publishing success! Unlock the potential of NFTs and blockchain technology with "Top Ten Reasons an Authors Should Use NFT and Blockchain.

Top Ten Steps to Build an Engaged Reader Community

Top Ten Steps to Build an Engaged Reader Community is the ultimate guide for authors who want to connect with their audience and create a supportive network. Learn how to define your target audience, master social media engagement, start a captivating blog, offer exclusive content, interact with readers, host virtual events, collaborate with other authors, create a compelling newsletter, encourage user-generated content, and show appreciation. With proven strategies and practical advice, this book empowers you to cultivate a supportive and enthusiastic community around your writing, propelling your author career to new heights. Don't miss out on this transformative opportunity!

The Non-Fiction Nexus: AI and the Future of Writing

Numerous enterprises have leveraged literary works spanning across eras to steer their Artificial Intelligence down the path of comprehending human existence, with a more distinct focus on crafting top-tier human-like prose. In the realm of education, AI has ingeniously generated an array of refined intellectual compositions. This leads us to ponder: "Should AI replace non-fiction writers?" "The Non-Fiction Nexus: AI and the Future of Writing" delves into both the advantageous and adverse facets of this query, shedding light on the AI perspective. The book explores the current AI landscape in writing, offering a glimpse into the present state and a tantalizing peek into the potential future.

Narrative Nexus: The AI Dilemma in Fiction

Numerous enterprises have leveraged literary works spanning across eras to steer their Artificial Intelligence down the path of comprehending human existence, with a more distinct focus on crafting top-tier human-like prose. In the realm of education, AI has ingeniously generated an array of refined intellectual compositions. This leads us to ponder: "Should AI replace fictional writers?" "Narrative Nexus: The AI Dilemma in Fiction" delves into both the advantageous and adverse facets of this query, shedding light on the AI perspective. The book explores the current AI landscape in writing, offering a glimpse into the present state and a tantalizing peek into the potential future.

Character Chronicles: Crafting Depth and Consistency in Creative Projects

Are you a creator of literature, film, TV, theater, or gaming? Craft characters that leap off the page and screen! "Character Chronicles" is your ultimate guide to mastering character development.

"Character Chronicles" is more than a book; it's your key to character mastery. Whether you're a pro or a newbie, this resource elevates your storytelling. Don't settle for two-dimensional characters. Enter the world of "Character Chronicles" and breathe life into your creations. Transform your projects with unforgettable characters that captivate your audience. Start your character journey today!

Navigating Amazon Publishing: A Comprehensive Guide for Authors

Are you an aspiring author seeking to publish your work? Amazon offers a wealth of opportunities, but it's essential to navigate this vast platform with a clear understanding of its strengths and potential challenges. In "Navigating Amazon Publishing," we provide you with valuable insights into why many authors choose Amazon and the factors you should weigh before making your decision.

Top Ten Challenges for Indie/Self-Published Authors: Navigating the Road to Success

Are you an indie author determined to thrive in the competitive world of self-publishing? Dive into the invaluable insights offered by "Top Ten Challenges for Indie/Self-Published Authors: Navigating the Road to Success," your essential guide to conquering the hurdles that indie authors face on their publishing journey. From finding your audience and unlocking marketing magic to building credibility and mastering quality control, this comprehensive guide empowers you to navigate the challenges of self-publishing with confidence. Learn to transform financial challenges into opportunities, master time management, defy stigma, and discover the secrets to effective marketing and discoverability. Don't let these challenges hold you back; embrace them as stepping stones toward your indie publishing success. "Top Ten Challenges for Indie/Self-Published Authors" equips you with the knowledge and strategies to conquer these obstacles and emerge as a triumphant indie author. Your journey begins now!

BOURGEOIS
MEDIA & CONSULTING

B Alan Bourgeois has an extensive track record of having helped hundreds of authors achieve their publishing goals through a variety of channels, including self-publishing and hybrid models. He is skilled in guiding authors to literary agents that are aligned with their specific needs.

Leveraging his extensive experience in book marketing and sales, as well as his participation in numerous book festivals, library conferences, and writing conferences, B Alan Bourgeois can assist authors in identifying and selecting the most suitable events to advance their careers. He further represents his clients at these conferences through his various organizations.

B Alan Bourgeois' consulting services are available to authors at every stage of their writing journeys - from beginners to seasoned professionals seeking new avenues for growth.

If you are interested in benefiting from his expertise, please complete the form below and he will promptly contact you to discuss your needs and how he can assist you. His first 15-minute consultation comes at no charge, and his hourly rate begins at $150 with the added benefit of discounts for purchasing multiple hours at once.

It should be noted that the recommended consulting duration for new authors is approximately 3-5 hours, whereas more experienced authors may only require 1/2 hour-2 hours of consultation time.

To schedule a consultation, please visit the authors website at: http://bourgeoismedia.com/index.php/consulting-service/consulting-service-2

Printed in the USA
CPSIA information can be obtained
at www.ICGtesting.com
LVHW011809050224
771025LV00040B/243

9 798869 138057